CU00704404

Confessing our sins

Confessing our sins

Nicolas Stebbing CR

Community of the Resurrection

Mirfield

Confessing our sins by Nicolas Stebbing CR

Quotations from Scripture are taken from
the *Revised Standard Version* of the Bible.

ISBN 0 902834 22 3

A CIP catalogue record for this book is available
from the British Library.

Printed in England by Page Bros (Norwich) Ltd.

First published in 2002 by
Mirfield Publications
House of the Resurrection
Mirfield
West Yorkshire
WF14 0BN.

Contents

Introduction

The story of Jesus begins in each of the Gospels with the Baptizer John. He is an extraordinary figure clothed in camel hair and burnt from a life in the desert. He preaches "Repent of your sins. The Kingdom of God is at hand". That is how Jesus also begins his ministry. He is one with John, calling people to repentance. From the start the Gospel has been concerned with sin. Yet this does not make it a miserable Gospel. It is full of good news. Part of that good news is that we can get rid of sin. Jesus takes it away. God forgives it. Yet still we sin. Even though we are baptised and believing Christians we sin and this sin drags us down. So the Church has always offered us the sacrament of confession. From the earliest years people have come to priests, to bishops, to holy monks and nuns, to fellow Christians and asked for help. They have received help through advice, prayer, example and the forgiveness which Jesus himself said his church could give.

In the western and eastern Churches the sacrament of confession has always been a central part of the serious Christian life. Of course it has often been misused and often misunderstood, but for many it has been the gateway to heaven. In the Anglican church it remained in use after the Reformation, but in a much reduced form. It sprang back into life in the mid nineteenth century and has been with us ever since.

Yet in recent decades there has been a falling away. Many reasons may be given for this, but partly there has been a change in our understanding of sin. Some sins which used to have a high priority are little regarded now. Others have taken on a new significance in the light of a much wider knowledge of the world and the destructive capacity of humankind. This little book tries to respond to this change of view. I believe, along with a great company of other Anglicans, that the sacrament of confession is a central and important part of our Christian life. I long for others to find in it the grace and strength which I have done. I would like those who suffer from guilt, from uneasy consciences, from sin which they can't get rid of, to discover in this sacrament the means of healing which God has provided for them.

Many people have helped in the making of this book. Fr Antony Grant CR read the whole script and made many suggestions for changes, most of which I accepted. Fr John Gribben CR gave me the main idea for Chapter Four and Fr Michael Boag has prepared the manuscript for printing. Above all, I owe a debt to the students of the College of the Resurrection, whose generosity, honesty and sensitivity in confession has taught me more than any book ever could.

Mirfield, Epiphany 2002

1. Who can be forgiven?

And he told this parable to some who trusted in themselves that they were righteous and despised others, "Two men went up into the temple to pray, one a Pharisee and the other a tax collector. The Pharisee stood and prayed thus with himself, 'God I thank thee that I am not like other men, extortioners, unjust, adulterers, or even like this tax collector. I fast twice a week, I give tithes of all that I get.' But the tax collector standing far off, would not even lift up his eyes to heaven but beat his breast saying, 'God be merciful to me a sinner!'" (Luke 18.9–13)

This is a strange story and an uncomfortable one. The tax collector was not a good man and he knew it. The Pharisee was good. He was virtuous. He did all that the law commanded and more. He was generous with his money and prayed constantly to God. He knew that his virtue was not all his own work and thanked God for it. Yet, as we know, he did not gain Christ's approval. He was proud. He despised those who did not reach his high standards. It is easy to see the point of the parable but as soon as we try to apply it to our own lives we find it difficult. Who is the Pharisee? Who is the tax collector? We would like to gain Jesus' approval. We would like to go from our prayers knowing that we are acceptable to God, and that our prayers have been heard. To do that we have to admit that we are like the tax collector, we have sinned.

It is rather easier to identify with the Pharisee. We are like him. We are part of that small minority who go to church regularly, who say our prayers, who try to keep the commandments, who give to the Church and to Christian Aid. It is difficult for us not to feel a certain contempt for the person who spends Sunday morning lying around doing nothing; or even the person who only occasionally turns up at Church instead of coming every Sunday as we do. We don't have to search ourselves very far to find that we say just the same sort of things as the Pharisee—and so are excluded from the Kingdom of Heaven. Actually that is not quite how it works. We exclude ourselves from the Kingdom of Heaven. Nobody prevents us from coming in, but the Kingdom of Heaven is only for those who see themselves as the tax collector did, and can say from the depths of their heart, "Lord, have mercy on me, a sinner."

At the beginning of every Eucharist we are invited to say that. The priest asks us to call to mind our sins. Then we say a form of confession and receive a form of absolution. In itself that is a very good thing and without that confession we certainly should not go to receive the Body and Blood of Christ. We are never worthy of receiving Holy Communion.

Only as self-confessed sinners can we be admitted. Only as people who know we are sinners can we be taken into the body of Christ and be seen in Him and not in ourselves. But if we are honest, how many of us really spend time before Communion thinking of our sins? How many of us say that confession with real penitence and sorrow? How many of us feel a great shame at our sinful state and a great longing for forgiveness, for absolution, for the certain knowledge that God has put aside all our sins and looks on us with love.

It is for this reason that Christ gives us what is called a sacrament in the Church. John's gospel tells how, when Jesus rose from the dead he met his disciples in the Upper Room, breathed on them with the Holy Spirit and said, "If you forgive the sins of any, they are forgiven. If you retain the sins of any, they are retained." (John 20.23) Now this was an amazing thing for him to say. We remember how, when a paralysed man was lowered through the roof to Jesus, Jesus said to him, "Your sins are forgiven you." (Luke 5.20) The bystanders were shocked. Sin is committed against God, therefore only God can forgive sin. If Jesus could forgive sins then he must be God, and Jesus proved he was God by raising the man from his sickness. Jesus really could forgive sins on behalf of God because he was God. Then he gave that authority to his disciples. That power has remained with those whom the disciples appointed to succeed them in the Church. A priest can forgive sins on behalf of God, not because he is specially good but because he has been given that authority.

At first in the history of the Church this authority to forgive sins was used mostly for people who committed public sins which caused great scandal. Since they were public sins which everybody knew about they had to be repented of publicly in front of the whole congregation. Then the priest would give absolution (say that the sin had been forgiven) and the person was restored to the body of the Church. Everybody knew he had been forgiven and had to be received back into their congregation as a restored brother. This was very important. Jesus spoke of the lost sheep whom the shepherd went after and found and brought home rejoicing and adds, "there will be more joy in heaven over one sinner who repents than over ninety-nine righteous persons who need no repentance." (Luke 15.7) Elsewhere Jesus speaks of what should be done if a member of the Church does something really wrong which puts him outside the company of Christians; "Tell him his fault between you and him alone. If he listens to you, you have gained your brother." (Matthew 18.15) All this made it clear what a terrible thing it was to lose a brother or sister from the Body of the Church and how wonderful it was to bring them back; but they could only come back if they repented. Before God we can only tell the truth. We cannot belong to a

Christian company on the basis of a lie. The tax-collector told the truth, that he was a sinner and so he was acceptable. He showed that he did not wish to be a sinner and even if he still continued to be a sinner his longing not to be a one made him acceptable to God.

As time went on Christians came to see that there was yet more to sin than this. Not all sin is public. Sometimes it is done very privately, but still continues to do great harm. If such private sin is confessed publicly it could created greater scandal and do great harm. If a man committed adultery and then had to stand up in front of the congregation and his wife and confess to it, this might break up his marriage, shame his children and hurt many other people. Yet he needs to be forgiven before God and needs to show that he really does regret his sin, and does not intend to do it again. So the Church made it possible for him to tell his sin only to the priest. If the priest believed he really was sorry he could then give him the forgiveness which he knew that God offers to all who are truly sorry for their sin. The man would be healed from the bad effects of his sin. He would be right with God, able to receive the grace of God to strengthen him in his wish to live a Christian life and no one else would be hurt. Of course this depended on the priest keeping his confession absolutely secret. Now instead of public confession of sin people had a form of confession that was so private that it took place only between the sinful person, God and the priest.

So far we have spoken mostly of public or serious sins—like adultery. Yet Jesus does not speak only of adultery as a sin. In fact Jesus amazed the Jews by the ease with which he forgave adulterers. The women taken in adultery, who should by Jewish law have been stoned, Jesus simply told, "Neither do I condemn you. Go and do not sin again." (John 8.11) He frequently said that tax collectors and prostitutes (the two groups that his contemporaries seemed to think were the worst kind of sinners) would enter heaven before even the righteous Pharisees. (Matthew 21.31) He is concerned with other kinds of sin—with hypocrisy, when a man says he will do God's will and gains credit for that, but in fact doesn't; or for that judgemental attitude which condemns other sinners without recognising that we ourselves are sinners. And St Paul takes this much further by listing as sins such things as "impurity, passion, evil desire, covetousness… anger, wrath, malice, slander, foul talk". (Colossians 3.5–7) Some of these sins are obviously destructive in a Christian community. Others seem to be entirely secret but are equally destructive because they tend to cut us off from each other. Inwardly critical, divisive or jealous attitudes make us despise or resent other people. Paul knows that they too will destroy us if we do not repent, and say we are sorry, and do all we can to turn away from them.

When the Christian Church came to understand this they realised what a huge thing sin was, and how it infected everybody from highest bishop to most recent convert. "All have sinned and fall short of the glory of God." (Romans 3.23) So all must repent and be forgiven. All must receive that grace of God's love which strips away all sin and restores them to the Christian body in the state in which God wishes them to be. So it was that private confession, to a priest, in secret, confessing all our sins (not just ones we think are big, but all of them) became the usual way that people prepared themselves to receive Jesus in Holy Communion.

Confession among Anglicans

Many Anglicans think that confession is only practised by Roman Catholics. This is not at all true. Confession is central to the practice of Orthodox Christians. It is a recognised part of the Lutheran tradition. It has always been part of Anglican practice, even after the Reformation. The Caroline divines were strong on confession. Dr Samuel Johnson regularly went to confession before Communion. It is true that the practice of confession almost died out in the eighteenth century but it was revived by the Oxford Movement in the nineteenth century and has remained a valued and much used sacrament ever since.

When should we go to confession?

It depends on how you look at it, and you can go for many different reasons. It is good to go before receiving a major sacrament of the Church. So before confirmation, ordination or marriage would all be good times to show God that we really mean business, that we want to be completely free from sin when we start on this new phase in our Christian life, that we want nothing to stand in the way of the grace which he is offering us. Most of all we want to receive this sacrament as a gift from him. A gift suggests a giver and we know that this Giver loves us more than we can ever hope to love Him. At least we will want to show that our love is big enough to make us want to reject anything that gets between us, Him and others, especially those we love; anything that suggests we do not really want to love Him.

Another time that we should want to go to confession is when we have got caught in some really serious sin, a sin that really weighs upon our conscience and damages our life with God. In the *Book of Common Prayer* the priest, when visiting the sick is told "the sick person shall be moved to make a special Confession of his sins, if he feel his conscience troubled with any weighty matter. After which Confession, the Priest shall absolve him." Clearly when we are sick and are wanting to receive God's grace for healing we should want to restore the relationship we have with God to its fullest degree of love. Yet also at other times the Prayer Book recognises that we need this ministry. When preparing to receive Holy Communion a person may realise there is sin on his or her conscience which cannot easily be got rid of. For this reason, the priest is told to say, "if there be any of you, who cannot quiet his own conscience herein, but requireth further comfort, or counsel, let him come to me or to some other discreet and learned Minister of God's Word, and open his grief; that by the ministry of God's holy word he may receive the benefit of absolution." This does not mean just the sins that society regards as being serious—like murder, adultery, or robbery, which perhaps not many of us do. Broken friendships, spiteful remarks, dishonesty in handling money, and many other things can make us feel very guilty, rightly so. The sacrament of Confession is there to help us with these problems. It is silly to go around carrying a load of guilt which God does not want us to carry. We feel depressed, angry, weary, bored with Christianity even, because this guilt is acting like a virus sapping our energy, taking away our knowledge that God loves us. We don't want to go on feeling like this. We need only admit that we were wrong and ask to be forgiven and the sin with its guilt is taken away. Then freedom, love and joy return.

In some Churches—the Orthodox for instance —people always make their confession before

Communion to ensure that they never fall into the sin which St Paul describes in 1 Corinthians 11.27 "Whoever eats the bread or drinks the cup in an unworthy manner will be guilty of profaning the body and blood of the Lord". The result is that they only go to Communion once or twice a year but prepare for it with great care. In the West most people who receive communion at all do so much more often than that, but often with very little preparation or thought as to whether we might "eat or drink judgement" on ourselves. (1 Corinthians 11.29) One way we can try to meet this need to prepare for Holy Communion may be to go to confession at least before the major Feasts of the Christian year. Easter and Christmas are two obvious occasions when we are already filled with amazement and gratitude to God for his generosity towards us. Ash Wednesday, at the beginning of Lent has always been a day of fasting and penitence and is a day we should consider very seriously how much we need the period of Lent to prepare for Easter. Other occasions, such as Pentecost, Michaelmas, anniversaries, or even our birthday might be good occasions to consider our relationship with God, and attempt to set it right.

Finally, there is the excellent practice of making confession regularly as a part of one's normal spiritual life. Once a month, once every six weeks or four times a year we set ourselves to examine our lives closely and then seek the forgiveness we know we need if we are to live our Christian lives to the full. For many people this is the occasion on which they receive spiritual direction—that is, talk with a priest whom they trust about their Christian life and prayer and seek advice on problems or questions that are bothering them.

How do I do it?

If you've not been to confession before it is best to find a priest whom you trust and are happy to talk to. You can then make an appointment for your confession. Or you can go to any priest who has a regular time when confessions are heard in a church. The actual sacrament is quite simple. Beforehand you need to write a list of the sins you can remember. For a first confession this may take some time. It is important to tell everything and certainly not to leave anything out deliberately through shame or a desire not to shock. This would suggest you are not really sorry, not sorry enough to endure a little shame, and would mean that you don't really love and trust God enough to be completely open with Him. You don't want to be like the Pharisee and keep a few things covered up to make yourself not seem a really bad sinner. You try to bring everything to God's light if you want to put sin absolutely and completely away. But there is no need to go into unnecessary detail, and if you honestly forget something it does not matter. That is taken care of by the rest of the confession.

When you go to confession you will probably find the priest sitting next to a prayer desk at which you can kneel. Ask for a chair if you prefer to sit. Just kneel down, or sit, quietly and wait for the priest to give you a blessing which will probably go something like:

"May the Lord be in your heart and on your lips that you may rightly and truly confess your sins to Almighty God."

You then continue with a form of confession which may go:

"I confess to Almighty God, Father, Son and Holy Spirit, and before you, my father, that I have sinned very much in thought word and deed by my own fault. Especially I remember these sins .... For these and all my other sins which I cannot now remember I am truly sorry, firmly mean to do better, humbly ask pardon of God and of you (father), advice, penance and absolution. Amen."

The priest will give a little advice and then suggest a penance for you (usually a psalm or a prayer which serves to show that you have received the forgiveness God is offering) and will then give you absolution. When he has finished simply leave. It is over and there is nothing more to do but live the Christian life free from the past and with joy towards the future.

At first sight confession may seem a very gloomy or miserable sacrament. In fact it isn't. It deals with some very sad material and for that reason it is necessary to look to the past. But the purpose is to free us from the evil of the past and turn us towards the future. It opens us up to experiencing the Resurrection of Christ. It shows us still more about the wonderful God we have who takes such care of us and showers us with gifts of love as soon as we give him the chance. And if it sounds like a horrid thing to do, to admit we are sinners and tell another person our sins, the experience of most people who have done that is that it turns out to be really joyful. We stop dragging our guilt around. We stop living a lie. We stop pretending there is nothing wrong. We discover the truth about God and with a bit of luck we enter into the joy of the angels in heaven over this one sinner who has repented.

2. The Father

When he came to himself he said… "I will arise and go to my father and I will say to him, 'Father I have sinned against heaven and before you, and am no longer worthy to be called your son; treat me as one of your hired servants.'" And he arose and came to his father. But while he was yet at a distance his father saw him and had compassion, and ran and embraced him and kissed him. (Luke 15.18–20)

That well known passage from one of the best loved parables in the Gospel goes to the heart of the problem most of us have about confession. We do not understand the father's love. The prodigal son did not understand it. That is not surprising. He was a self-centred, dissolute young man whose only concern in returning to his father was one of self-interest. He wanted something to eat. He had done a great injury to his father. He had told his father, "Give me my inheritance." That was almost the same as saying, "I wish you were dead". He had then wasted that part of his father's hard earned wealth. He had disgraced the family with his behaviour and if he had bothered to think for a moment about his father he would have realised how anxious, distressed and hurt his father would be about this young son who had disappeared into the seedy life of pleasure in foreign towns.

There is no hint of that kind of repentance in his decision to return. Yet his father treated him as if he was penitent. Or rather the father in his love didn't bother about asking all those questions about whether he was sorry. He simply ran out, embraced him, kissed him and set up a party for him. He swept aside his speech, his excuses and simply showed him his love. If this were a historical story we would hope that the boy finally saw how much he had hurt his father and allowed the father's generosity to pierce the hardness of his heart and teach him to love his father in return with something like the love he had received. Sadly we know that prodigal sons and daughters exist all over the world who regularly exploit their parents' love while learning nothing from it. Are we not like that with God? Have we any real idea of just how much he loves us, and how much it costs him to love us as steadily and as fully as he does? Let's start at the beginning. He created us. "The Lord God formed man of dust from the ground, and breathed into his nostrils the breath of life." (Genesis 2.7) Even if we now believe that the actual way man was created was in some evolutionary manner we can still say that we are created by God; each little particle in our bodies was made by him; every breath we take depends on him. How can we dare to think we live our lives apart from him when we would not have life at all, or bodies, or anything, unless he had given it to us. Then we look around us we see a world created by God "Out of the ground the Lord God made to grow every tree that is pleasant to the sight and good for food" (Genesis 2.9) No one who has studied creation can fail to be amazed at its complexity and wonder. There is so much beauty to look at—rivers, sunrise, flowers, valleys, animals, stars and moon; and when we try to understand it our minds cannot take it in. Worlds, galaxies, universe occupy a space beyond anything we can imagine and are held together in a complicated system which stretches our mathematics and science to breaking point when we try to unravel its mysteries. At the minutest level, too, the world of atoms, neutrons, particles and their relationship goes on fascinating scientists as they attempt to understand it. Yet we men and women are greater than all this. We are more complex in our structure, have more potential for change and growth; uniquely, as far we can tell, we have free will and a freedom to change which nothing else does. God appears to have created us as the highest point of his creation and given us a world that is beautiful and fruitful. Yet we ransack it for its riches, exploit the other people of God to our advantage and fail even to notice the beauty God has set before us.

"The heavens declare the glory of God and the firmament shows his handiwork" cries the psalmist (Psalm 19) and God placed us in this wonderful world, giving us freedom. He gives us, also, the ability to grow constantly in acquiring knowledge, to learn the skills we need so that we can survive and enjoy the world He made. How have we used this freedom? There is a heart breaking poem in the prophecies of Isaiah: "My beloved had a vineyard on a very fertile hill. "He digged it and cleared it of stones and planted it with choice vines;… he looked for it to yield grapes, but it yielded wild grapes." (Isaiah 5.1–3)

The prophet goes on to describe the injustice, the suffering, the bloodshed which takes place in this world he has made. We do not need to look very far to see what a mess we have made of the world, and how often that mess is not just caused by accidental foolishness but by greed, by selfishness, by ignoring the feelings or the needs of others. These are the sins which may seem small to us, but which lead to the destruction of peoples, to the rape of the countryside, to global warming, massive erosion, expulsion of whole nations from their land, the flight of the poor to the desperate poverty of the cities.

How does God feel as creator? It is a strange mother who does not feel love towards her child—the child she bore within her for nine months and gave birth to with pain. It is a strange artist who does not love the painting he has produced, who does not care when the work is defaced or destroyed. God is both mother and artist. He is the most perfect of both. His love for us, his creation, is closer and stronger than that of the best of mothers or the most passionate of artists. How does he feel when we turn away from him, ignore him, think we have made ourselves, damage the work he has done in us, destroy the works of art he has created around us? If we really understood the nature of God's love as creator we would feel so bitterly ashamed that we would crawl away and live with pigs in shame and disgust at our behaviour; except, of course, that is not what God wants. He wants us to come home. Our question may be, do we really want to go home? The prodigal son didn't want to go home. He probably would have preferred to go back to his life in the cities, but that way was closed to him. He went home only because he had no choice if he didn't want to spend the rest of his life among pigs. It was not love for his father that took him home, but simple need. That is not a bad reason for going home. We will return to that. Yet how much easier and joyful it is to go home when there is someone who loves us, waiting for us. Our first task is to admit that we really have wandered far away from this Father who loves us. We may not be living among pigs. It might be better if we were because we would be more desperate then to get away. Yet we have a past, and that often clings to us refusing to let us go, not wanting us to go to the Father. More recently we have sinned steadily in small, almost unnoticeable ways which have led us with small steps away from God. Our second task is to realise how much he wants us back, not to punish us but to delight in us and to shower us with the gifts of his love.

Let us return for a moment to the world God created for us. With all its dangers, its rough edges, its diseases, wild animals, earthquakes and wicked people, it is a beautiful world. We never get tired of its beauty. No two sunsets are ever the same. Every spring comes new and fresh even though we have seen it many times before. Skies and clouds, food and drink, warmth and invigorating cold make this a wonderful world to live in. And God has given it to us. He has set us in the midst of it. A gift implies a giver, and almost always a giver is one who loves us. The more we look at the beauties of this particular gift, the more we shall see the love behind the hand of our God who gives it.

We may feel the same about the people who surround us, our family, our friends. We did not make them. We love them but we cannot claim credit for them. Even parents generally recognise that their children have personalities of their own. When they turn out well we can only be thankful. No parent can ever force a child to turn out well. When we fall in love, if it is true love, we are always amazed that such a wonderful person can suddenly come our way. We are even more amazed if they return our love. How can such a wonderful person love me? That love is a gift and can only come from the God who is love, because he wants us to have it.

Then there is ourselves. Unless we are sick we all love to be alive. We don't want to be dead. Life is a wonderful thing, constantly rising up inside us.

My heart leaps up when I behold
A rainbow in the sky…

said Wordsworth, and it is that leap of the heart which makes us love to be alive. Sometimes, of course, we feel depressed. Sometimes we don't like the way life has turned out. Sometimes we wonder how we go on—but we do go on, hoping the joy of life will return. When it does we are glad. Joy, life, love, beauty—all of these are gifts from God. How can we doubt that God loves us when he has given us gifts. Yet what have we done with the gifts?

We all know what it is like to have our love rejected. When we were young and first fell for a boy or girl at school, how often that got nowhere! The other person ignored us, was rude to us, told us to get lost, or didn't even notice we were there. That is terribly hurtful. How hurtful it is when we give someone a present—a present, perhaps, we have spent much money on, chosen with great care, wrapped up and given with a vulnerable anxiety; we so much want it to show our love. And the other person says, "Oh I don't want that." Or makes a polite remark and puts it on one side. Or a few days later we find the present that summed up our love broken or given away. That makes us weep, and the pain goes right through to our heart. Yet is not that what we do with the gifts God has given us?

If we think through the story of our lives we find that we have done this over and over with God.

Usually we did not mean to, but that does not make it much better, when God sees his gifts of love thrown away, ignored, broken. We see how vulnerable God has made himself, offering us these precious gifts, when he knows how weak we are, how likely it is that we will not understand and will throw the gifts away, or even think that we have made them ourselves. If we see any of this truly we shall be appalled. Every sin, be it even a momentary disregard of God's love, will appear horrible, ungrateful beyond belief. We will be sickened and ashamed. We will feel remorse and know that nothing, nothing we can ever do will make up for that horrible rejection of God's love. Nothing will make it go away. We may find ourselves with Peter on the banks of the Sea of Galilee when he suddenly realised that this teacher he had had in his boat, and perhaps treated quite rudely, was really from God. He fell down at Jesus' knees and said, "Depart from me, I am a sinful man, O Lord." (Luke 5.8) Our only desire may be to go away in shame and hide, like a sick dog, like a child who knows he has disgraced his parents. That is not what God wants. He wants us to come home.

We really do need to see just how aweful every sin we ever commit really is, since each is a rejection of that love. We will feel wretched, ashamed, disgusted with ourselves, if there is any decency in us at all. Yet we must never forget the truth that is greater than our sin, that God's love for us never goes away.

Simply because it is so huge, so constant, so unfailing, nothing we do can ever drive it away. No matter how dreadful it is we can always go back, as the prodigal son went back and find God waiting for us, running to meet us, flinging his arms around us. The wonder of it is that the more we see how appalling our sin is, the more amazed we shall be by the depth of God's forgiveness. It becomes almost a joy to have sinned so much, to discover that God loves us so.

Can a woman forget her sucking child,
that she should have no compassion
on the son of her womb?
Even these may forget,
yet I will not forget you.
(Isaiah 49.15)

3. Jesus and Sin

The scribes and the Pharisees brought a women who had been caught in adultery, and placing her in the midst they said to him, "Teacher this woman has been caught in adultery. Now in the law Moses commanded us to stone such. What do you say about her?"… He said to them, "Let him who is without sin among you be the first to throw a stone at her… When they heard it they went away, one by one, beginning with the eldest, and Jesus was left alone with the woman. Jesus looked up and said to her, "Woman, where are they? Has no one condemned you?" She said, "No one, Lord." And Jesus said, "Neither do I condemn you; go, and do not sin again." (John 8.3–11)

One of the extraordinary gifts Jesus had was that of changing the perspective on events, shifting the ground so that those who were trying to catch him out got caught out themselves. The scribes and Pharisees here had tried to catch Jesus out. If he agreed with the law of Moses and they stoned the woman he would be regarded by many as a murderer. If he disagreed with Moses he would be condemned as one who did not keep the Law which God had given. Jesus shifts the ground. He neither agrees with Moses, nor denies him. He turns the question back on the accusers themselves. Is any of them free from sin? Are they not also caught up with this woman in the state of sin that infects the whole world?

Our modern age does not like talking about sin. Perhaps that has always been so. In every age people have found ways to disguise sin, to pretend it doesn't exist. So today we try to pretend there is no such thing as sin. We admit we have weaknesses, but we say we can't help those. We know we do things the Church disapproves of, but say "everybody does it, so it must be all right". We accept society's view that if something we do does not obviously hurt another person then there is nothing wrong with it. Or we simply disagree with the teaching of the Church and insist that something we like doing is not a sin because we enjoy it.

Even if we do admit that there are many sins that we do not like and agree that we should not do them it is easy to believe that really and truly they do not matter very much. They are small sins. They don't really do any damage. Does it really matter if I enjoy a little gossip? or don't bother to say my prayers? or make a racist joke? or avoid talking to a person I don't like? Why does the Church make such a fuss about sin? Well, it is because Jesus made quite a fuss about sin. It is true that his idea of what was sinful was quite a lot different from some of the people of his day. Yet he talked a great deal about sin. If we look honestly at the Sermon on the Mount (and it is curious how many people say they love the Sermon on the Mount but insist that no one could live like that today!) we will see that there is a great deal about sin. If we want to take Jesus seriously we have to take sin seriously. If we want to deny the awefulness of all sin, we shall have to deny Christ.

Yet Jesus catches us by surprise. The woman has been caught in sin and Jesus refuses to condemn her. It's not that he doesn't care about adultery, but what he cares about even more is healing. Jesus hated illness. He hated the evil which leprosy brought to people's lives; he hated the sight of a man with a withered arm, a woman bent with infirmity, a child in epileptic convulsions. So he healed those people. He is angry with the demons who seemed to have caused this illness, angry, too, with the self-righteous Jews who thought it was a punishment for sin, or thought he should not heal, do good, on the sabbath day. Yet though Jesus hated sickness he did not punish people for being sick; he healed them. So too, he hated sin, but he did not punish people for being sinners. He forgave them. His concern was, and remains, the present, not the past. The past is necessary. The sinners needed to admit they were sinners, then Jesus could release them from their sin, concerned only for the future, that they should not sin again.

Even today, when medical science has established that most sickness is caused by viruses, bacteria, defective genes, unhealthy life styles and other identifiable causes there remains an area of guilt. Some sickness is still caused by behaviour which is sinful. In other ways there appear to be links between people's awareness of guilt and their vulnerability to illness. Certainly if we wish to receive God's grace in healing our physical illness we shall need to ask ourselves whether unrepented sin is preventing us from receiving that grace.

In the gospel story it is easy to imagine that Jesus feels a great sadness, or perhaps an anger, not with the woman but with the self-righteous crowd which brought her. They did not realise they were sinners. They had never looked at themselves. Or they thought that their sin could be dealt with by the odd sacrifice in the temple, which changed nothing of what was actually in their hearts. Jesus looks into their hearts and asks them to do the same. We do not know whether they did. Did they creep away in shame when they realised that they too were sinners? Or did they just realise that they could not claim publicly to be without sin and not be accused of pride?

It is easy for us to condemn those Jews. Yet Jesus himself did not condemn them; just as the prodigal son's father did not condemn the older brother. That story can be uncomfortable one for good faithful Christians to read. We have not behaved like the younger son. We have not left our work, our home, to live with prostitutes and end up with pigs. We may sometimes wish we had. We may resent the fuss made of a new convert, perhaps a known sinner who comes into the Church and seems to think that his past is all forgotten. We may be glad he or she has repented but still feel that we ourselves are rather better, more deserving of attention, more reliable as Christians than the newly arrived are. Then we find ourselves sympathetic to the older brother who will not come to the party and tells his father "These many years I have served you, and I have never disobeyed your command; yet you never gave me a kid that I might make merry with my friends."(Luke 15.29) That is mean and self-centred. He will not enter into his father's joy. He will not rejoice with his brother, preferring him, perhaps, to remain far away with the pigs. He shows that he really resents his years of faithful service. It has not been a service of love, born out of gratitude to a father who has always cared for him. It has been a service of duty, reluctantly undertaken, self-righteously performed. Now he is found out for his meanness and selfishness. Yet even so, the father says no word of criticism. "Son, you are always with me, and all that I have is yours." Nothing could be more generous than that. Not for a moment does he condemn. Jesus is not here to condemn, and nor are we. It is easy for us to speak out strongly against the sins we are not involved with: the drug dealing, the theft that goes with taking drugs, the sexual licence that leads to AIDS, to pregnancies, to marital breakdowns. We may even go further and denounce those who take huge salaries, or avoid paying taxes, or fiddle the trusts they are looking after. Yet do we consider ourselves? Do we realise that Jesus does not ask us to condemn other people's sin, but to recognise our own?

That will not be easy. We lack practice. We live in a society that trains us to look at other people's wrong doing and never our own. We don't know what sins look like other than the ones that are held up and screamed about in the daily newspapers. There are many others the newspapers are not concerned with. They are just as destructive because they are well hidden. Until we find them and admit they belong to us, we cannot receive the forgiveness that Christ wants to give us. We are like a sick person, walking round insisting he is perfectly well. He can't get better till he admits he is sick and looks for treatment. When he gets the treatment and is cured life is transformed. He finds he is filled with life, with energy, even with joy. The medicine may have tasted nasty; the surgery may have been painful, but the result is life beyond anything he had dreamed of. The older brother needs to see his sinfulness as much as the younger one did, but it will be hard for him. It is easier to stay blind and keep it all hidden. Unlike the younger brother he remains dead and is lost. His mean spiritedness and self-centredness prevents him coming back to life. Is that what we faithful, practicing Christians really are?

What happened to the crowd in the Gospel story? We do not know. We hope they went away ashamed, and not angry, and that their shame led them to concern themselves with their own sins, and be sorry for them and turn away from them. What happened to the woman? Again we do not know. It is easy to imagine her relief. She had been in real danger of death. Now she was safe. Was she touched by Jesus' mercy, or his compassion? Did she realise that here was a man who really understood and cared for her? Again we do not know. It is not our concern.Our concern is to read the story and see whether we are like those people in the condemning crowd, and if we are to repent.

So let's be honest. If we find we are in situations like that and we realise we are one of the crowd, what is our sin? In the first place we have lost sight of the woman. She has sinned but she is still a person, a child of God, loved by God. We need to see her as such and to love her, hard as that may sometimes be. Our first failure is that we don't care about her. Yet God cares. Should not we do the same? We have become mesmerised by sin. We have seen the wickedness of it, the destructiveness of it, and have become like it. We think that by denouncing someone else's sin, we've distanced ourselves from it. We shout out, I'm not like that, so as to drown out the whisper inside which says, "That's exactly what you are." We have wanted to destroy rather than to heal.

Our second failure is that we have forgotten we really are sinners. Our sins may be different from those of the people we want to condemn. They are still sins. St John tells us, "If we say we have no sin we deceive ourselves and the truth is not in us."(1 John 1.8) A careful reading of the Sermon on the Mount will show us that what John says is true.

In this story we have seen how Jesus caught everyone by surprise. The woman obviously expected some terrible punishment. Instead she found compassion, understanding, forgiveness. The crowd thought they would see Jesus discomforted, or themselves proved right. They may have looked forward to some violence, some justified expression of anger. Instead they discovered they were sinners. That may have led them to anger and denial, or perhaps made some of them repent—and change their lives. Surprises are often very uncomfortable, but when they come from Jesus they turn out to be full of life. Confession can turn out like that. On a human level alone that is not surprising. We have all known occasions when we have admitted we were wrong in something and found it led to greater understanding, to new levels of friendship, to self knowledge and to freedom. As long as we live with lies we are crippled by them. Facing the truth frees us from the deception of pretending that all is well. We can't enjoy friendships based on lies for long. We need the truth. We can't relax with ourselves if we do not know our own truth. Our own truth does not turn out always to be bad. Often we hide the best part of ourselves because we think that other people won't like it. We try to be tough, unemotional, secure and say the things which people around us say in the hope of being like them. But people around us are often wrong. When we stop pretending we are tough, and let emotions appear, and say what we really believe is right we show our true self. "You will know the truth" says Jesus, "and truth will set you free." (John 8.32). This confused the Jews as it confuses us. "We have never been in bondage to anyone. How is it that you say, "You will be made free'?" Jesus replies "Everyone who commits sin is a slave to sin… If the Son makes you free, you will be free indeed." (John 8.36)

It is the presence of the Son, whom we call Jesus or Christ, that makes all the difference. Confession is more than a human exercise, good as that may be. It is a sacrament, a place where we meet Christ. This is where the real surprises lie. Christ turns out to look different when we come to him in this way. He also become more real, as we do. We also begin to see God his Father more truly as he is. Sin blinds us. It is like a cataract over our eyes, distorting what we see. Our tears soften that cataract and Christ takes it away. We will not see much or everything when that first happens. We may remember the blind man whom Jesus healed who said at first he saw men "like trees, walking" (Mark 8.24). God will always be a surprise to us, every time we look at Him, but confession makes it possible for us to see him more truly as he really is. That may be exciting, or challenging, or alarming, or even uncomfortable. It will never be dull.

4. Confession as a Sacrament

Four children are exploring a rambling old house and find a battered wardrobe. They climb into the wardrobe to hide from the adults; as they move backwards they suddenly discover they are in another land—the land of Narnia. It is a world which exists just beyond the world we know. It is not a world of children only. Grown up Narnians are there. Terrible things happen there. But it is a world that only children can reach from this world. It is related to our world but the contacts between the two worlds come mainly through Aslan, a lion in Narnia; Someone else in our world.

When C.S. Lewis wrote the enchanting Narnia stories he touched on one of our great hopes and secret longings, that this world is not all there is and that the other world which we are told exists after we die is accessible now, at least sometimes, in some form. What he describes we recognise in the sacramental world—not just in the seven sacraments which are offered to us in the Church, but in the whole sacramental understanding of Christian life in which the things of our world are the means by which God's life is given us. Our world looks firm and solid, prosaic and ordinary, and unromantic. But it only needs a little push, a different perception, a movement from outside to show that another world is there and we can briefly move into it, or it into us. Our world is God's world. He created it as he created us. Since he created this world he can use the things of this world to make himself more real to us. So water, bread, wine, oil become the means by which God himself is brought to us, and makes himself accessible to us. He chooses to do this. We do not magic him into existence. We do not manipulate or control the movements of God. He comes to us, creating those thin spots in the veil of eternity through which he can pass, or through which we can go to catch a glimpse and experience for a moment the joy that will one day be ours.

When Peter, Susan, Edmund and Lucy go into Narnia they change their clothes; they breathe a richer air. They become kings and queens. They are capable of more than they ever could do or be in England. So with us, when we move into the world of sacraments we set about creating a sacred space in which different things can happen; and a sacred time in which we become something more. It is a mistake to see confession simply as a sacrament that prepares us for other things. It is part of a new world, a world that has come into our world. Every sacrament is a sacred place happening in a sacred time. Each sacrament is a sanctuary set aside for God. It is not that God is not elsewhere; nor can he be imprisoned in a sanctuary, but a sanctuary becomes a special kind of world of more than make believe, in which the believing really does come true. We behave differently there. We dress differently. We treat things with reverence—candles, water, vestments, books, people—a reverence which has nothing to do with what they are in themselves ("Bowing down to wood and stone"—some would say) but everything to do with what they represent, and how God has chosen to use them to come to us himself. We kneel before bread and wine as if it were the greatest person we could know, because somehow the God of heaven will come to us, has come to us through that bread and wine. For we "have come to Mount Zion and to the city of the living God, the heavenly Jerusalem, and to innumerable angels in festal gathering…"(Hebrews 12.22) We kiss a book of ordinary paper and words, because those words reveal to us something which is of such value, filled with such life that our hearts go out to it in thanks. It does not matter what outsiders think of these curious rites. They do not believe though they may want to. This world is not real to them. To us it is startlingly real and changes the nature of everything else.

Sacraments do not simply have a significance for the individual who receives them. They are part of the means by which the world is renewed. The world which God created has fallen with man. The whole world groans for salvation (Romans 8.22). As God uses the very stuff of this world to come to us his creatures so the world itself is taken back into the economy of God and begins to become what it was always intended to be. When we receive the sacraments we are working with God in the redemption of the world. Nothing about the sacraments is ever entirely individual. However each one of us may cherish those moments of grace when we receive Communion, or hear the words which absolve us of our sins, we are part of a world which is infinitely larger than we are. Confession seems at first to be such a personal, individual thing. In fact it touches every member of the Body of Christ. Our sins infect the Christian body. When we reject our sins and allow Christ to heal the effects of them we drive that bit of evil out of the Christian body and allow God's presence in. In a world where there is so much evil our sacramental turning from evil to God in its way affects the whole world. It may be the most effective prayer we can make on behalf of this suffering world.

In each sacrament Christ is to be found. A sacrament is not a thing, not a parcelled up dollop of grace. In each sacrament we meet the whole Christ. It changes the way we think of a sacrament if we remember this. At Baptism, as the water splashes over the child it brings that child into the hands of Christ and hands it on to the Father. In Communion it is not an inanimate body of Christ that we receive, but a living person who comes to meet us in those fragments of bread and wine. We have come "to Jesus, the mediator of a new covenant, and to the sprinkled blood that speaks more graciously…" (Hebrews 12.24) In confession we do not mutter our sins simply into the ears of a human priest, but into the presence of the loving Son of God through whose Spirit we are restored to the Father who longs for our repentance.

We believe in a Risen Christ, but we sometimes find it difficult to explain what that means. Yes, he did rise from the dead—but what does it mean for us now that he is alive in the world? In part it is just this, that we keep meeting him in the sacraments, particularly in those two, communion and confession, which we can receive often. He is always unexpected, yet comes to us with joy:

I kiss my hand
To the stars, lovely-asunder
Starlight, wafting him out of it; and
Glow, glory in thunder…
For I greet him the days when I meet him, and bless
when I understand.

wrote Hopkins. We can't guarantee that we shall always feel Christ there, but we know he is. And from time to time it happens, and we suddenly do understand what is going on and joy rises up in our hearts. This makes us realise that we can't live our daily life separate from our sacramental life. The Christ I meet when I receive Communion will go with me from the church and I must answer to him. The Christ who assures me that my sins are forgiven because he has embraced me with this love, goes with me when I meet the people against whom I have sinned; he encourages me to pray again when I had confessed I had found it hard. No; a sacrament is not a 'thing'; it is a moment in which I meet a Person. Receiving sacraments brings us into a relationship which leads us to heaven.

Sacraments do not only involve Christ. "When the Spirit of truth comes... he will glorify me, for he will take what is mine and declare it to you. All that the Father has is mine..."(John 16.13f) Every sacrament brings us the Holy Spirit and takes place through his presence, giving us what the Father wants us to have as inheritors of the Kingdom of his Son. And a sacrament cannot take place in isolation from the Church. Every sacrament takes place in the Church and we are built up with our fellow Christians and learn to love God through loving them. Baptised once into this Body which is Christ we draw life constantly from the Christ whose life we now share. In this the barriers of time fall away. We recall the story of the Passion, of the Last Supper, of Jesus on the road to Emmaus; and then as the liturgy tells us on Maundy Thursday, "We know that it was not only our ancestors but we who were redeemed and brought forth from bondage to freedom, from mourning to feasting. We know that as he was with them in the upper room so our Lord is here with us now..." It will help us then to realise how God is present to us in confession. I kneel next to a priest, but I am not alone. Christ kneels with me, praying for me to his Father as he prayed for me once upon a Cross. The Father is just there in front of me receiving my confession with love, compassion and understanding. And the Holy Spirit is around me and within me searching out the recesses of my heart, exposing the sin, bringing it forth and allowing his presence to heal the torn places that the sin has left. Each confession takes me into the heart of God and there I find love.

At the heart of Christianity there is a mystery and it is the mystery of love which is founded on the mystery of the Cross. "Lo, I tell you a mystery..." says St Paul (1 Corinthians 15.51) and he speaks often of the mystery of Christ. The mystery of the Cross is that there, in the worst place that there could ever be, when the perfect Son of God in whom was no sin at all was crucified by the hatred and sin of men, where the life of the eternal God was smothered in death, where love such as we have never known was rejected and scorned, still love was revealed. Still love can be found in the heart of that wickedness and in the heart of wickedness wherever we find it. No sin is ever too great to exclude the mystery of God's love. No shame, or pain, or despair that we suffer can ever deprive us of the love of Christ. Just as the Cross became for men and women ever since the road of glory into the heart of God, so our own sin becomes the way we pass through the Cross into the love of God.

5. Healing the World

"And I, when I am lifted up from the earth,
will draw all people to myself." (John 12.32)

Jesus died for all the world, not just for a part of it. He was not only concerned with the Jewish people, or with his own followers. He died for everyone. Very early in the Christian Church's history there were various attempts to limit salvation to one special group of people—Jewish Christians, perhaps, or groups whom we now call Gnostics, or Roman citizens, or people of better classes. Always these attempts have been resisted, by St Paul, St Peter, St Augustine, St John Chrysostom and thousands of other great Christian leaders. All people are created by God. All men and women are children of God. God offers salvation to all of them. Whenever Christians try to limit salvation to a special group (and sadly, they go on doing it) they deny that God loves all that he has made. That is blasphemy since it tries to limit the love of God who cannot be limited. This is important to our exploration of confession. It means that when we come to prepare for confession we need to look very widely at the way our life has touched the lives of all the people of God. There is always a danger that Christianity should become individualised, privatised. We live in a world which says that religion is a private affair. That sounds tolerant, but it also makes religion into a kind of hobby like stamp collecting, or a belief like that in flying saucers, which may just possibly be true but will have no influence at all on the way we live our lives. It is often because of this that people find confession irrelevant. We may look at the traditional sins, the way we relate to those close to us, the way we do or don't say our prayers and feel at the end that we haven't really touched on anything important. We feel, if we go to confession often, that we are just saying the same things every time and nothing much is changing. We may be unaware of any inadequacy in our confessions but just see them as a private affair between us and God concerned mostly with how we pray, how we go to Church and how we get on with our families. Christian life is concerned with much more than that. God is concerned with much more than that. Throughout the Scriptures we see God calling his people not to think that religion is just a matter of private devotion, or of being kind to our families. The Jewish people were always falling into that error. They offered sacrifices. They kept the law in their own house. But God said they must do much more than that.

> *Render true judgements, show kindness and mercy each to his brother, do not oppress the widow, the fatherless, the sojourner, or the poor; and let none of you devise evil against his brother in your heart. (Zechariah 7.9–10)*

Or again,

> *Woe to those who devise wickedness*
> *and work evil upon their beds!...*
> *They covet fields and seize them;*
> *and houses and take them away. (Micah 2.1–2)*

We may reply we do nothing like that, but then we look at our society, of which we are a part, from which we benefit. There is no question that our society does all of that both in this country and outside it. This is what is called structural sin. A great deal of evil is simply built into our society. Poverty and unemployment leads to drug addiction and crime—not always, but often enough for there to be a very clear connection. If we ourselves are not poor or unemployed, do we bother about those who are? Do we vote at elections in a way that may change the structures that keep certain groups of people always poor and unemployed? Or do we vote simply for our own advantage?

We all know now that large parts of the world are exploited by the rich Western nations. Investment in other countries often means simply importing from those countries at prices which are wickedly low in order to sell at a large profit in England or America. All of us feel we have a right to buy what we want as cheaply as we can; but if this means men and women in South America or India must starve and their children have no education do we not have a responsibility to use our purchasing power to ensure they are better paid?

We all see in our newspapers and on television news how many conflicts there are in the world, where people are dying, often in very large numbers. In Asia, the countries of the Pacific Ocean, much of Africa, South America and even in Europe in the Balkans or Northern Ireland we see people killing each other. Do we know how often they are using British guns? How often British weapons are used for torture and oppression? The British arms industry is a major source of British wealth. This is a complex issue. Britain may have a right to defend itself and may even be right to assist other countries in legitimate defence, but arms easily multiply and get into the wrong hands. The temptation to make money is not easy to resist. All of us who live in Britain (or America, or France) benefit directly or indirectly from this trade. Do we care? Can we think about it? Can we at least confess to God that our hands are not clean and that we need his wisdom and help to see what we can do?

Once we realise we have a responsibility for the arms trade we shall see that we cannot ignore the effects of other aspects of our trade. Ours is an affluent country but our wealth is built on other people's poverty. These people cannot afford to live, cannot educate their children, cannot get a fair wage or fair price for their produce because the people who arrange the trade to our advantage keep them in poverty. Even the earth's ecology is thrown out of balance as forests are destroyed to supply the greedy West and the atmosphere is damaged by the industrial processes from which we benefit. Is this too big a problem for individuals like us to have an effect on? In fact it is not. Fair trade organisations, pressure on politicians and a willingness to pay the difference all has an effect which we cannot ignore if we are really to show we care for all the people God loves and the world he created and gave to us to look after. Jesus told us, "Blessed are those who hunger and thirst after righteousness..." That means, to care about these kind of issues. If we do not care about them to the extent of hunger and thirsting after them we are failing God.

A different way of understanding the real nature of our sin would be to look imaginatively at the Church. We know it is the Body of Christ and that all Christian people are part of it. What happens to a body when a part of it is diseased? It hurts, or is sick, or functions badly. It does not need to be a very big part of the body for the disease to be deadly. We live in the body of the Church. What is the effect on that body of our little sins, our meanness, our selfishness, our gossip, our jealousy? Such sin does not only infect us. It infects everyone around us. We need to see our sin as an infection and realise how we spread disease. We would think twice about bringing measles, or chickenpox into a group of people we care about, yet we bring our sins and they help to make the Church the sluggish, uninspired, often sinful institution it so often is.

St Paul, in one of his striking metaphors, compares the Christian body to a loaf of bread. A little bad yeast ruins the bread.

> Your boasting is not good. Do you not know that a little leaven leavens the whole lump? Cleanse out the old leaven that you may be a new lump. For Christ our Paschal lamb has been sacrificed. Let us, therefore, celebrate the festival, not with the old leaven, the leaven of malice and evil, but with the unleavened bread of sincerity and truth.
>
> (1 Corinthians 5.6–8)

Again, when we come to prepare for confession we may admit that we haven't prayed much, have missed occasional services, have failed to read the Bible—and then wonder if it really matters. Christians are expected to pray, to go to Church, to read the Bible. If we don't, will anyone be much worse? Is it simply a rule that we can break if we don't feel like keeping it? If it is simply a rule then we probably shouldn't be keeping it. Rules have great value so long as we see them as ways to help our love grow stronger. In a marriage we may have a personal rule to make certain specific offerings of love, always to do the washing up, or bring our spouse a cup of morning tea in bed and we know this will be appreciated and will help the marriage along. Such rules have meaning and work; but a rule which has lost its meaning needs to be revised. The rules we make about praying, reading the Bible or going to Church are all intended to show our love for God, to help that love to grow and to give God every chance we can to work with us, turning us into the kind of Christian people he wants us to be. We need to keep our eyes fixed on the real purpose of the rule, then we will see the nature of the sin, if there is a sin in breaking it. Some rules can be broken without sin. If we don't read our bibles because we have been sick, if we don't say some prayers because we have been to evensong, if we genuinely have such a busy day that we simply cannot manage anything at the end of it then we can trust in a loving God to understand. However, if our days are always so busy that we can never pray we may have to change the way we work. If we find we have broken our devotional rules we need to ask ourselves why? Was it genuinely unavoidable? Or were we lazy, or too self-centred, or simply forgot about God.

In this case we need to remember that our prayer is not just for ourselves. It is not to make us happy or to improve us as people or to get us what we want. Our prayer is first for God. We give glory to God, and turn our love towards God when we pray. We take part with him in the salvation of the world. We become part of the living constant prayer of the Church. Other people need our prayers. Other people who are weak, or sick, or doing the work of Christ in lonely or dangerous places rely on our prayers. The world needs the Church to pray. Ours is a world where wickedness seems to grow constantly. As a war is stopped in one place two more break out in others. As social conditions improve in a country problems such as drug addiction and crime can get worse rather than better. Christians try harder and harder to bring people into the Christian faith and yet we see that our society turns steadily away from God. The Church and the world need our prayer, both as intercession for their needs, and as praise, offering the praise to God that they can't offer. When we fail in our devotional life of reading Scripture, or praying or going to Church our failure weakens the whole Body of Christ.

That can be depressing knowledge, but the good side of it all is that even our weak and faltering prayers are doing good in the world. We are not isolated creatures struggling along by ourselves. We may feel helpless at the sight of all the war, poverty, unbelief which comes to us in the papers but our prayer does reach out to those people in ways we can never know. Our time spent reflecting on Scripture enriches the body of Christ and may well lighten the heart of another brother or sister far away. When I take part in a eucharist I am offering a sacrifice for the whole world with Christ who offered his sacrifice on the Cross; and when I confess and receive forgiveness

I am letting go of my part of the sin which the whole Church bears. It may be the most effective prayer I can make for others who are caught up in sin and have not yet found the way to escape.

6. Sex

"You have heard that it was said, 'You shall not commit adultery.' But I say to you that everyone who looks at a woman lustfully has already committed adultery with her in his heart." (Matthew 5.27–28)

Considering how much time is given in Christian circles to talking about sex, and how often sin is identified almost entirely with sex, it comes as quite a surprise to find that Jesus himself hardly ever deals with the subject. Those who try to work out a Christian view of sex have a hard task to find more than a handful of texts in the Bible as a whole, still less in the gospels, which deal with it, and they are often ambiguous. Jesus does of course deal quite a lot with women who have fallen into sexual sin, either through adultery or prostitution. It seems he kept company quite often with them. He never denounced them as wicked. Instead he thought them rather better than the scribes and pharisees. That may have been a rhetorical exaggeration. Instead of condemning them he forgave them—as we saw with the woman taken in adultery (John 8.3–11) and the woman who washed his feet (Luke 7.36–50). This means he did not condone their sin, or tell them to continue with it. He knew they needed forgiving, but even more they needed to be loved, to be treated as human beings, to be set free not to sin.

Yet he had very high standards. Not only should one not commit adultery. Even to allow the thought to enter one's mind was adultery. We may protest that one cannot live anywhere in the world without seeing good looking men and women and we can easily let ourselves think how much more we would like to do with them; that much good literature includes very explicit sexual encounters; that advertising, films, television, other people's conversation pushes us constantly towards sexual activity. We can't get away from the fact that Jesus believed all sin (not just sexual sin) began in the heart and in the mind. He told the Jewish people:

> *What comes out of the mouth proceeds from the heart, and this defiles a man. For out of the heart come evil thoughts....These are what defile a man. (Matthew 15.18–19)*

If we think about it we will admit he was right. That is where we must begin to understand our own need to ask for forgiveness.

Yet there is a further problem. In the past (perhaps, though it is always easy to forget that people in the past had many of the same problems as we do) the Church took a clear and consistent line on sex. All sex outside marriage was wrong. This did not necessarily mean that all sex inside marriage was right. Contraception and other apparent interference with the natural process was (and by some still is) thought to be wrong. Even within a normal loving relationship sex was somewhat doubtful and only justified by having children. The *Book of Common Prayer* Marriage service says that marriage is "for the procreation of children... for a remedy against sin and to avoid fornication". Few people today would find that an adequate view of sexuality within marriage. Today we see things quite differently. Sex itself is given to us by God, not only for procreation but also for the enhancement of love. This sets a large responsibility on married people to ensure that their sexual relationship is really loving and does not make unacceptable demands on the other. Yet what happens outside marriage? If sex is an expression of love can it not always be justified by love? If love exists between two men or two women can they not express this sexually even though such relationships have never been allowed by the Church? If young people need to be at ease with their sexuality in order later to make a good marriage and be healthy and well integrated themselves, must they not explore and experiment and learn not to regard sex as an area of great darkness and danger only to be enjoyed under the tightest conditions of safety? Living in a world where sexual behaviour has so radically changed it is difficult for Christians to go on saying "No" to all these questions.

This chapter is not large enough to discuss these questions properly, but when we come to confession we cannot simply leave them out. If we are confused or unclear about the sexual situation we find ourselves in we need to talk about it with God; we need to open ourselves to his light and to the guidance of his Holy Spirit. Confession is a good place for that. A sensitive priest will be able to help us understand what is going on and even, perhaps, assure us that we have nothing to worry about. Here we can find the right sort of forum to explore these questions and consider not just what is right, but what God is asking of us. That is the crucial question. God calls each of us to a particular way of living and it is unique to us. Our relationships with other people are part of this call; our use of the gift of sexuality may be a vital aspect in understanding who we are and what God is offering us. Our sexuality tends to open up the most sensitive parts of our human nature and offers us both the opportunity for real growth and the possibility of great hurt, great damage.

What does this mean in practical terms? Well, if I am married I need to open up to God every aspect of my married life and consider whether it is truly loving or whether I sometimes exploit my husband or wife. If I am not married but am in a relationship of some kind the same is true. Am I using the other person for myself, or are we really seeking love? Are we growing in commitment and responsibility? If we are outside what the Church has always considered to be the right way of relating to others are we honestly dealing with this question or are we being persuaded simply by our own desires?

We men and women are almost always imperfect in what we do. We hardly ever get things completely right. This should not surprise us, nor is it really a negative observation. It is simply a fact of life. Sin is something we all suffer from and it tends to make things go wrong. None of us has yet grown to the fullness of what God intends us to be. Love and sex, friendship and the mere art of working together are all areas in which our imperfections will show. We need to be honest about these, look at them clearly, bring them to God either as sins to be confessed or as questions on which we need his light.

When we do this we find a God who is loving and compassionate, who understands us and wants to give us what we truly desire. Sorting out our true desires from the false ones may take time but it is an exciting process for here we are dealing face to face with God. Asking these questions generally brings us into a closer relationship with God and can open up new freedoms in our relationship with others. We may well discover that what we thought was sinful, or was considered sinful by others, is not sinful at all. We may find that what we thought we could not do without, we can and so discover that we were slaves to a kind of behaviour which limited us and denied us growth. We may discover that of course we have sinned, perhaps very much more than we had thought, but even that is not wholly bad news.

We remember what Jesus said of the woman in Luke 7.47 "Her sins which are many are forgiven, for she loved much; but he who is forgiven little, loves little."

Often one of the fruits of bringing our questions and problems about sex to God in confession is to find them transformed. What had been a problem about sex becomes an opportunity to love. Without leaving the physical behind we find a new dimension has been added in which compassion, understanding, freedom and a sense of giftedness change our whole experience of our life. The Holy Spirit has come down to us and led us further into love.

7. Penance, Advice and Absolution

In the standard form of confession amongst Anglicans the final words are a request for "penance, advice and absolution". Much is concealed under that simple request.

Penance is the first word that may cause people some alarm. It is not a word commonly used in English now and many of us may not even know what it means. If we do use it we probably use it in the sense of 'punishment'. People speak of doing some unpleasant task as a penance. In medieval times a penance often involved something really difficult like going on pilgrimage to Rome or giving a great deal of money away to the poor. In the sacrament of confession today a penance is more often a psalm or a prayer which the priest suggests as an act of thanksgiving for forgiveness. Sometimes the penance will be chosen because it refers particularly to some important aspect of a person's confession. It may be a reading from Scripture or it may even be a particular act we can do to make up for what was done wrong. The important thing is that it shows that we are genuinely sorry. That is what the Latin word behind penance means. "I am sorry". It also shows that we accept God's forgiveness and are grateful for it. Usually, too, we will find that the penance gives us hope and confidence that God really is the loving and compassionate God we have been told he is. The penance helps us to realise that our confession really has been accepted and God's forgiveness has come to us freeing us from the past and making it possible to live hopefully and joyfully in the future.

The request for advice is also very important and raises a number of issues here. We come to confession primarily for forgiveness and the forgiveness we receive through the priest is from God. We must never lose sight of the fact that the main aim of this sacrament is God's forgiveness. However, most of us find sin a problem. We promise we will not sin again, but if we are honest and realistic we know we probably will. We have bad habits. Some sins are so habitual that we do them almost without thinking. Others come from the people we work with, the life style we choose to live. Some come from ignorance. Some, like not praying properly or failing to come to Church may happen because we are trying to pray in the wrong way, or at an awkward time. Other sins, perhaps of getting angry with our family or neglecting important work may occur because we are over stressed and have just taken on too much. Most priests are (only too!) experienced with this sort of problem. It is helpful to talk through these areas with someone who is not going to judge but will really try to offer help.

We may also find ourselves with questions about Christian life which are not to do with sin. Now is a time we can ask them. However, this raises the question of what is appropriate in time of confession. If we are kneeling, or if there are other people waiting we don't want to get involved in long chats! However, in recent years many people have realised they need some one with whom they can talk about their Christian life. They may call this person a spiritual director or a spiritual guide, or a soul friend to make it clear that it is a relationship in which the two people together seek to understand what God wants. The rôle of spiritual director is not a rigidly defined one. Spiritual direction may take place in confession, if it is not too long. Some people may prefer to find a spiritual director who is not their regular confessor, even perhaps someone who is not a priest and so cannot give absolution. Sometimes people make a regular practice of talking for an hour or so with their spiritual director before making confession—so that both sides then know what is behind everything that is confessed. There are many different possibilities and all are acceptable.

However, one important thing to realise is that spiritual direction is not the same as counselling—certainly not therapeutic counselling. What it provides is an opportunity to explore the way God is working in my life and to try and see whether God is inviting me to move on or to understand something in a new way. Often the director is able to shed light on our problems from a wider experience. Most importantly, just the fact of being able to talk in confidence to someone we trust helps us to understand things better for ourselves. At any rate it is always good to talk and to listen. What the priest says even if we disagree may trigger off something from God. The spiritual fathers of the earliest Christian tradition always insisted it was good to bring all our thoughts and temptations out into the open. As long as we keep them hidden we cannot find out if they are bad. If they are bad they will fester and rot. When we bring them out before God, either in confession or in spiritual direction, God is able to shed his light on them and they will be shown up in their true nature—good or bad. Often the mere light of God will simply make illusions and false fears fade away.

A spiritual director will also be a great support to us in our Christian journey. He or she will pray for us, encourage us, support us and sometimes challenge us. In this way God will find more and more opportunities to lead us on to greater things. However, it is important not to let spiritual direction replace confession. If the director is not careful it can simply become an experience of fireside chats, increasingly centred on self and not on God. To be really healthy and God centred spiritual direction really needs confession in which we continue to acknowledge our weakness and our failure, and where we unambiguously appeal to God, the centre of our life, for absolution.

What is absolution? Technically it means "to set free". Sin binds us. It binds us to bad habits. It drags us down and stops our souls reaching out to God. It dampens our enthusiasm and makes it impossible for us to feel the joy of God, to experience the hope which God promises us through Christ or to know his love. Sin makes us feel we are unlovable. It makes us feel God is far away and not interested in us, or wants only to punish us. Absolution frees us from all that. Absolution lets us dare to hope. Absolution opens up a future for us. It shows us that God does care about us, and will set aside even the very worst of our sins so that we can come to him. That is freedom indeed. Of course absolution is not magic. We are still weak people and we need to cooperate with God in every way we can in order to overcome our sin and to make full use of the grace he offers us in the sacraments. In absolution the Holy Spirit comes to us, refreshing our weary spirits, strengthening our will, giving us that hope of new life without which we quickly despair and give up. This may make us feel as if we are at the beginning of a journey, very excited and full of energy. Or we may feel rather like an invalid who has just come out of hospital, better but lacking in strength and not at all sure the healing is going to last. We may even feel very little different at all. That doesn't matter. God works at a level which is much deeper than feelings. We look ahead to this journey we shall make with God. He is with us and now that we have been freed from sin he can work in us. If we give him the chance he will show us the freedom that is open to us in all kinds of ways we never suspected. We will find we are free to look on Christ and find him guiding us through the difficulties of our daily life. We may find that prayer becomes increasingly attractive as a time we give specifically to being with God or we may find ourselves increasingly conscious of God's action and presence in our daily lives. The words from a lovely hymn may become our prayer:

> Heal our wounds, our strength renew,
> on our dryness pour thy dew,
> wash the stains of guilt away.
> Bend the stubborn heart and will
> melt the frozen warm the chill,
> Guide the steps that go astray.

Holy Communion itself gains in significance as a time when we know we are receiving Christ into ourselves.

Sadly, we will sin again, almost certainly. In one sense it doesn't matter. By now we shall have discovered that God really can be trusted to forgive us our sins. All we need to do is ask. Each sin becomes an opportunity to discover more of the grace of God (though as Paul warns us in Romans 6.1 that is not a good reason for sinning!). Absolution will open our eyes to the many more ways in which we are failing to live up to our Christian calling. We may feel we are getting no better. In fact we are growing in grace and self knowledge; knowledge too of the ways of God. Absolution does not (or should not) make us feel pleased with ourselves, complacent or self righteous. It does increase the hope in us that God is very near and that he will see that we do not fail to enter his Kingdom in the end. For this reason we will want, and need, to come back again and again to confession and enter once again into God's compassionate love.

8. Should I go?

If you have come this far and are asking that question, the answer is probably "Yes". You should go to confession. However, you needn't go in a rush. We need to give ourselves time to understand, as far as we are able, what we are going to do. We need time to turn our attention away from ourselves, to God. If this is a first confession we will need quite a lot of time to think over our lives and bring God everything we can find that we want to have healed and taken away. God does forgive everything, even the things we honestly forget. Yet we will want to do as thorough a job as we can in presenting ourselves to him in all our honesty and sorrow and longing for his love. The more completely we can confess, the more deeply we will know that God's healing grace is entering into us. It is almost as if we make space for God, by digging deep inside and tearing out sins by their roots, emptying the cluttered, dirty rooms of the house (to change the metaphor), throwing away the things we don't want to hang on to. God enters those places in our lives and begins the long, slow work of change. It is sometimes painful. Good things often are painful, but we quickly realise that we are being brought into a new relationship with God. We are changing inside. Life is taking on a new meaning but new meanings can often be disturbing. That disturbance is a sign that good things are happening. It isn't a sign to stop but a signal to go on. Sin is a confusing business and until we have spent quite a long time trying to understand what is going wrong in our lives and repenting of it we will find it difficult to think about.

One major difficulty most people have about confession is to wonder what the priest will think of us when we confess sins which may seem terrible to us; or we may be afraid we are wasting time with sins that look trivial and silly. It is important to remember that every priest who hears confessions goes to confession. He will know how much he himself has needed the compassion and understanding of another priest to hear his own sins. He will know also how costly it is for us to say out the things of which we are really ashamed and so he will receive our confession with respect. He will know that no sin is ever trivial if it has the power of keeping us away from God. It is not his job to judge, or to rebuke, or to punish. He receives our confession and shows us the merciful forgiveness of God.

At the same time every priest is bound by the seal of the confessional. That is absolute. He or she must never and may never say anything of what is heard in the confessional to another person. He must never mention it even to you unless you raise the matter yourself. He should not even think about it. Most priests actually get very good at forgetting what they hear. He certainly must not allow it to affect the way he thinks about you. Actually priests who hear confessions usually find themselves very moved by the honesty and integrity of a costly confession. When we meet the real person in confession telling the absolute truth about themselves in humility and sorrow we see the real person whom God loves and find ourselves sharing in that love.

We may learn an important lesson about a priest's rôle in confession from the Eastern Orthodox. In the popular mythology of the Eastern Church there are many stories of angels coming down to earth to take the priest's part in all of the sacraments, except confession. Angels cannot do this since they are not human. A priest shares in the humanity of those who come to him. He too is a sinner and as a sinner he can enter into their sin and can assure them that they, like him, are forgiven sinners. He too lives in penitent love, knowing he is fragile, knowing he is the way of ministering inexpressible graces to God's people, taking them up to the very throne of grace itself. What he hears does not take place in this world. That is why he cannot speak of it outside the confessional. They are words between you and God. The priest who hears this knows that they have no place outside the confessional unless you choose to give them place. It is not a mere formula for the priest to say at the end of confession, "Go in peace. God has put away all your sins. And pray for me, for I too am a sinner." In this the priest needs to be like the tax collector in Luke 18.13 who "standing far off, would not even lift up his eyes to heaven, but beat his breast saying 'God, be merciful to me a sinner!'" Otherwise he should not dare to minister the reconciliation of God.

What happens after the first time? Different people have different practices and certainly have different needs. It is a sad truth that none of us is ever free from sin for very long. The greatest of saints were aware of their failure to love God as he deserves to be loved and to give themselves with generosity to the people of God. There was once a desert father who was noted for his holiness. As he approached death he became increasingly distressed. "I want more time to repent" he said. Those with him said "Surely father, you have spent your life repenting." "No," he said, "I feel I have hardly begun." We cannot pretend to be better than the saints. At times we may feel that there is little for us to confess, but that usually means we have let our sight grow dim and our conscience become hardened. Confession will teach us to look at ourselves with increasing knowledge and growing sorrow, but also with increasing joy as we find again and again that the love of God is waiting for us and enters us precisely through the points where we see our sins against him. Sorrow opens the hardest places of our heart to the Holy Spirit and he teaches us to love. We also only find how lovable we are when we have let God and another person see the worst we know about ourselves and find that still they love us.

We need a discipline in this matter of how often we go to confession. If we leave it to our own feelings human weakness, or the devil, will prevent us fulfilling our good intentions and gradually we will drift away. A good discipline is to go to confession four times a year, particularly at the major feasts. Christmas, Ash Wednesday and Easter are appropriate times and makes it possible for confession to be part of the joyful celebration of the Feast. It is a fitting preparation to make our Easter or Christmas communion in a state much closer to that we would like to be in always, whenever we receive the Body and Blood of Christ. Michaelmas or the Feast of Our Lady in August would be a good way of breaking up the long run of Sundays after Trinity with a renewal of our longing to serve God with every fragment of our hearts and minds. Confessing our failure to do just this acts as a prayer that we really will be turned to God and be filled with his grace and life.

How should I prepare?

Start with prayer. Ask God simply to show you where your life has fallen short of the love which he wants for you. Then it is usually helpful to read some scripture. The story of the tax collector in the temple (Luke 18.13), the woman washing Jesus' feet (Luke 7.36–50), the prodigal son (Luke 15.11–32), or the crucifixion itself will help us to turn our minds to God and realise what we are really doing in confession. Some people also find it helpful to ask someone very close to them to tell them what they may not have seen. This can be a costly but healing bit of reconciliation within the family which can be a very good preparation for confession.

It is then best to get a large piece of paper and start writing. If this is a first confession you may need to divide your life up into periods such as childhood, adolescence, student days, marriage and the last year or two. For the earlier periods it is not necessary (and anyway impossible!) to remember and confess everything. Yet we know how tenacious the human memory is and how things we have done wrong decades ago can continue to eat away at our minds. We need to look carefully and see if there is anything like that still holding us back, turning us away from God and preventing us from living Christian life to the full. It may seem trivial; it may be horribly serious. If it troubles us it needs to be offered to God. The general rule is that if we remember definite sins from the past we must confess them. That is the surest way of showing that we really are sorry and want to be freed from them. We may have to do a bit of digging round in our memories to make sure there are not events that need bringing out into the open, though pain and shame have encouraged us to hide them for many years. But if we honestly forget things and only remember them after confession, that is no matter. They can be left behind.

When we look at the more recent years, or the time since our last confession, it is usually helpful to spend some time with certain passages of Scripture. The Beatitudes (Matthew 5.1–12) are excellent for this purpose. So too is 1 Corinthians 13. Especially for a first confession it is best to write down exactly what we are going to say so that nervousness or shame does not make us suddenly tongue tied. Having it all written down beforehand takes quite a lot of the pressure off and helps us to make our confessions in a calm and thorough way. However, there is no rule about this. We are talking to God, not making some performance. We need to do whatever makes us feel we are being true to ourselves and God.

When St Paul wrote to the Corinthians he got very angry with them for their sinful behaviour, and as he said "I made you sorry with my letter". Yet he does not regret this but says "I rejoice, not because you were grieved, but because you were grieved into repentance… For godly grief produces a repentance that leads to salvation and brings no regret, but worldly grief produces death" (2 Corinthians 7.9–10) Christian repentance is not backward looking and does not lead to the kind of despair that drives people to suicide. Christian repentance turns life around. It produces a change of heart. It allows the Holy Spirit to enter the deepest places of our life and give them new life. Christian repentance is not centred on self but centred on God. It changes our life and as long as we can keep our attention away from ourselves and turned to God sin will find it difficult to enter our lives. Instead of despair a deeply rooted joy and an unquenchable hope fill our hearts. That is the joy felt in heaven over one sinner who repents rather than ninety-nine righteous people who think they need not repentance. (Luke 15.7)

9. *"Blessed are those..."*

In the early centuries non-Christians could not understand what made Christians so happy. They were a persecuted minority, often excluded from society by their strange beliefs. They worshipped a man who had died on a Cross. They were usually from the poorer parts of society. They did not seek power, or wealth. They avoided many of the pleasures that everyone else thought were natural. And yet they were happy. When arrested they seemed confident nothing bad could happen to them. When tortured they were brave, even the young. When threatened with death they were often filled with joy. What caused this amazing joy that survived all the pain and disadvantages of a hard life in a hostile society? Christians themselves said it was due to two things, intimately related. The first was the Resurrection. They knew that Christ had risen from the dead. They had a real awareness of Him present with them in their lives, especially when life was hard; and they knew that death would open up to the hope of life for ever with this Jesus who had appeared so wonderfully on earth. The second cause of their joy was that they had already found themselves freed from sin. That great burden of sin which had tied them to the past, which had made it so impossible to do anything good, even when they tried, had been taken away. Their immediate experience of Christian life was that sin and all its sickness had left them. Now they were free to hope that the future would bring them the fulfilment of all the promises Jesus had made. "Rejoice and be glad, for your reward will be great in heaven…" is how the Beatitudes end. That is a promise we need to take seriously. The odd thing about the Beatitudes is that they turn our experience upside down. In a way that is what confession does. We recall our sin, that most unpleasant and shameful part of our life and come out in joy.

Blessed are the poor in spirit…

Most of the people around Jesus were poor— economically poor and without power of any kind. Jesus often warns people that riches will prevent them entering the Kingdom of God. How attached are we to our riches? Does our work get in the way of worshipping God? Are we so secure in our lives that we do not need to trust God for anything? Do we consider the poor, those whom Jesus said would be the first into the Kingdom? Do we learn from them? Do we help them in any serious and costly way?

Blessed are those who mourn…

Why should we mourn? It is for the state of the world. This world created by God, given to us, seems to have been taken over by evil. Men kill; children are starved, women are raped, land is destroyed, diseases like AIDS kill millions. Some of this is our fault. Some of it not. We mourn because the world is in such a mess and God's love towards us is treated with such contempt. The good news is that God will comfort us. The fact that we mourn for the world in its fall from God means that we will find ourselves specially open to the presence of Christ showing us how he is in fact working in the world to bring it back to God, and wants us to work with him. When we mourn we pray for a suffering world and make it a little more possible for God to come into that world through us.

Blessed are the meek…

…or the humble. This is not considered a virtue in Western society. We do not understand it. Our society expects people to be thrusting, aggressive and successful. When we meet real humility we are amazed. It is very attractive. The truly humble person is relaxed and secure because he or she has no illusions, no false expectations and does not cling to honour or long for respect. Such a person is genuinely interested in us; and is amazed at the goodness and wonder of God. "Having nothing, yet possessing everything" is how St Paul describes it. (2 Corinthians 6.10) Simply because the meek person claims nothing for his own he finds the whole world is there for his enjoyment. Free from the desire to possess riches and honour and power, the humble person finds she is taken up with God and finds the riches of heaven already at her disposal. How far am I from learning this kind of humility? Do I seek power? Do I assert myself over others? Can I really be proud before God?

Blessed are those who hunger and thirst
after righteousness

Righteousness is part of the nature of God. God's righteousness is mocked when we do wrong. When we see people treated unjustly we must be offended for their sake, but also for God's sake since his righteousness is being dishonoured. When we long for justice for the poor we are longing for God's will to be done. If we do not long for justice with that desperate hunger which thirsts as if we are dying in a desert, we have not learned really to long for God.

Blessed are the merciful...

Jesus often speaks of mercy and condemns those who do not show mercy—mercy to the poor who suffer if we richer people do not help them; mercy to those who hurt us. Do we forgive them? "Forgive us our trespasses as we forgive those who trespass against us" is actually about mercy. If we do not forgive we cannot be forgiven. It is easy for us to hold onto our resentments, our sense of being hurt, our anger with another person. As long as we do that we cannot come near Christ. He will show us our anger and resentment, our refusal to show mercy and ask us to forgive, so that we can be forgiven. Can we do that now?

Blessed are the pure in heart...

To be pure in heart means to seek God with all our being. Anything that turns us from God is an impurity of the heart. Worshipping in a weak and distracted way is a failure of the heart. Impurity comes, too, from ignoring the laws God has given us, of sexual integrity, of minds free from the spiteful, jealous, mean thoughts which make it impossible really to attend to God. Every sin, every kind of greed, every act of self-indulgence brings impurity into the heart. This corrupts our vision so badly that we do not even want to see God. We cannot see the attractiveness of God nor understand that to see God is the most wonderful experience we can ever have. If we don't desire God above everything else we have let impurity distort our innermost selves and are missing the point of all Christian life.

Blessed are the peace makers…

Sadly, most human life involves conflict; conflicts in families where people are always arguing, conflict at work where people are competing for power, conflict in Church where Christians keep trying to force their will on others; conflict in the world where nations try to gain more wealth than they need. Christ was the Prince of Peace. His presence brings peace into the conflict. In the Upper Room he said to the disciples "Peace I leave with you; my peace I give to you." (John 14.27) Christ is in us. We receive him week by week in Holy Communion. We are members of his Body. We believe he has risen from the dead to be with us. Do we create peace where we are; or do we cause conflict?

When Jesus appeared to his disciples after his Resurrection he said to them, "Peace be with you. As the Father has sent me, even so I send you… Receive the Holy Spirit. If you forgive the sins of any, they are forgiven." (John 20.21–23) This is his gift of new life, the forgiveness of sin. We need it and the world needs it. Peter knew this. When Jesus asked if he and the other disciples would leave him as so many other followers had left him Peter said. "Lord, to whom shall we go? You have the words of eternal life."(John 6.68) Those words of forgiveness free us from sin so that we can enter eternal life with Christ.

A Form of Self-Examination

1. Who can be forgiven?

Can I admit that, like the tax collector, I am a sinner and need the mercy of God? Do I feel that sin is poisoning my life? Do I really want to be freed from my sin? Can I pray this prayer with all my heart?

O Holy Spirit, fountain of all light,
pour your bright beams into my soul,
that I may see my sins as clearly as I shall see them
on the day of judgment.
Teach me, O holy God, both the evil I have done,
and that which I have caused.
Make me see how unfaithful I have been
in your service.
Make me know how often and how much
I have offended you,
how badly I have wronged my neighbour
and myself.
I ask this through Jesus
who died to free me from my sin.

2. The Father

Do I waste what God has given to me? Do I care about other people? Do I care about the world and the destruction of its resources? Do I spend time enjoying the beauty God has made? Or am I like the older brother, not caring that others have found new life; jealous of the attention a new convert gets? Do I feel that my long service of God means I am special? Am I ashamed to realise this? Can I pray now that God will show me just how I am like the prodigal son, or the older brother, and make me ashamed?

3. Jesus and Sin

Have I understood that God does forgive me? If I remember that I can think of the worst thing I have ever done and know I am forgiven. Yet still I need to admit I was wrong, and feel the sorrow, and want not to have done it. As I look into the forgiving eyes of Jesus can I feel that sorrow and wish I had never sinned? Or am I like the people who brought the sinful woman to Christ. Do I condemn others in their sin, and not realise that I too have sinned? Can I pray that God will help me understand sin so that I can see for myself how even apparently small sins can actually be really bad?

4. Confession as a Sacrament

Do I approach church as the sanctuary of God and try to find a new world there? Do I look on my fellow Christians as fellow citizens in the household of saints? Do I reverence the sacraments and let God work great changes in me through them? Do I put prayer above all other things in my life, or does it only get the left over bits of time when I have finished everything else? Can I pray now that God will change my whole life, and help him to do this by offering my sin?

5. Healing the World

Am I generous with what I have, or am I mean? Do I care about the poverty in the world? Do I try to do something about it? Do I vote for those who will consider the poor and the weak? Or do I live just in the world of my own and not care what happens to God's other children, elsewhere?

Lord teach me to see every person as my brother or sister, as they are each your children. Teach me to care more for them than I do for myself. Let me see what I can do to make life better for others and give me the desire to do it. Show me where I am centred on self, selfish and self concerned. Amen.

6. Sex

Can I think carefully about how I express the love I have for another person? Am I selfish, possessive, or self-indulgent in this? Have I simply taken the easy option, and accepted the standards of society? Will I admit that Christ expects more of us who follow him? Will I let him lead me in the expression of my love?

7. Penance, Advice and Absolution

Can I now look at my life as God looks at it? He is generous and wants what is best for me. This is not always what is comfortable. Sometimes I must make hardœchoices and give up things I do like. Yet also sometimes I am invited to take a step which is really exciting and gives me more than I ever hoped for. Can I look to God for guidance. Should I now talk with a priest, or with someone who I think is close to God and help me see what is the right thing to do?

8. Should I go?

What will life be like after confession? What can I hope for? If sin is taken away I will know God more clearly and be able to love him with more of myself. If I am free from guilt I will be able to look to the future with hope and confidence. If I have been thinking I am really rather a poor Christian I can hope that God will now be able to make me a more loving Christian. If I really want to enjoy the fruits of the Kingdom of God, I must go through this gate of repentance. If I want to show God that I really do love him, that my love is not just words, then I will want to do everything I can to set aside my sin and make things right between us, won't I?

Some useful Bible passages:
Luke 18.13
or Luke 7.36
or Luke 15.11
or an account of the crucifixion
or 1 John 1.8–9
or 1 John 2.1–2

A Prayer Before Confession

O my God, I am sorry for all my sins;
I hate them above all things,
because they deserve your judgement,
because they have crucified my loving Saviour
Jesus Christ,
and, most of all,
because they offend your infinite goodness;
and I promise to try,
by the help of your grace,
never to offend you again,
and carefully to avoid the occasions when I might sin.

A Form of Confession

The penitent kneels down and says:

Bless me, father, for I have sinned.

The priest says:

May the Lord be in your heart and on your lips that you may make a right and true confession of your sins.

Penitent:

I confess to Almighty God, to blessed Mary, to all the saints and to you, father, that I have sinned in thought, word and deed, by my own fault. Especially (since my last confession which was… ago) I remember the following sins…

For these and all my other sins which I cannot now remember I am truly sorry, firmly mean to do better, humbly ask God for forgiveness and of you, father, penance, advice and absolution. Amen.

After giving some advice and a suitable penance the priest says:

May almighty God have mercy on you, forgive you your sins and bring you to everlasting life. Amen.

Our Lord Jesus Christ, who has left power to his Church to absolve all sinners who truly repent and believe in him, of his great mercy forgive you your offences, and by his authority committed unto me, I absolve you from all your sins, in the name of the Father, and of the Son and of the Holy Spirit. Amen.

The infinite merits of our Lord Jesus Christ, the prayers of Our Lady and all the saints make whatsoever good you have done or evil you have endured to count for the increase of grace, the remission of sin and the attainment of everlasting life, and the blessing of God almighty, the Father, the Son and the Holy Spirit be with you now and always. Amen.

Go in peace. God has put away all your sin and pray for me, for I, too, am a sinner.